THE SHELTER

For Kate

CARYL PHILLIPS

THE SHELTER

AMBER LANE PRESS

All rights whatsoever in this play are strictly reserved and application for performance, etc., should be made before rehearsal to:

Judy Daish Associates Ltd.
122 Wigmore Street,
London W1H 9FE

No performance may be given unless a licence has been obtained.

First published in 1984 by
Amber Lane Press Ltd.
9 Middle Way
Oxford OX2 7LH

Typesetting and make-up by
Midas Publishing Services Ltd., Oxford

Printed in Great Britain by
Cotswold Press Ltd.
Eynsham, Oxon

Copyright © Caryl Phillips, 1984

ISBN 0 906399 49 1

CONDITION OF SALE
This book is sold subject to the condition that it shall not, by way of trade or otherwise, be lent, re-sold, hired out or otherwise circulated without the publisher's prior consent in any form of binding or cover other than that in which it is published and without a similar condition including this condition being imposed on the subsequent purchaser.

'Remember a shelter is a temporary place of refuge in a disaster. It cannot be like home.'

A message from Undro-pan-Caribbean disaster preparedness and prevention project. St. John's, Antigua.

(*Sign on the wall of the Ministry of Education, Health and Social Affairs. St. Kitts.*)

The Shelter was first performed at the Lyric Studio, Hammersmith, London on 1st September, 1983. It was directed by Jules Wright and designed by Tim Bickerton, with the following cast:

HER/IRENE	Kathryn Pogson
HIM/LOUIS	Rudolph Walker

INTRODUCTION

I have really never been able to remember the actual physical process of writing a play: it is an awful blindness I have come to categorize as literary amnesia. I have an idea, I worry, I become excited, I worry again, and then one day (in fact more usually one night) I try to enter into the piece and a few precious days are lost. Roughly speaking this is how I imagined *The Shelter* would come to be written for, despite only having two plays to my name, the game of creation was already becoming reassuringly familiar, though sadly no less frightening because of this.

And, as I sat down to try and write this play, the accustomed panic set in but this time it quickly multiplied, as in a gambler's nightmare, until many hours of work spawned little more than a few loose scratchings of dialogue that led precisely nowhere. I stopped, feeling I was shouldering an additional burden to those I was used to, such as form, characterization, dialogue and so on — a burden that was making it difficult, and might ultimately make it impossible, for me to continue this game. This supplementary burden I named 'responsibility'.

Much has been written about the responsibility that the writer has to himself, or to his theatre, or to his piece of work, or to his audience, or to his actors, or to his family and friends, or to his predecessors, or to those that will come after him, or to all of these things, or to none of them, or to any number of the permutations available within them; but I, perhaps motivated by the luxury of inexperience, had always felt that my only responsibility was to locate the truth in whatever piece I was working on, live with it, sleep with it, and be responsible to that truth, and that truth alone. After all, I could see no other way of surviving as a sane individual given the often cruel contradiction of the society I had chosen to live in. Criticism of myself and my work, often both at the same time, indivisible, except when it suited those criticizing, was always forthcoming, but one grows to live with ignorance, for others have suffered and still are suffering from fates far worse than mere wounded pride. But, when troubled and insecure, I have always looked to these words of the late Langston Hughes, who said it all and so much more besides: 'The negro artist works against an undertow of sharp criticism and misunderstanding from his own group and unintentional bribes from the whites.' This being the case, and it was and still is the case today (and probably will be tomorrow), the location of the truth, and a resultant quiet but grave determination to follow it through to its logical conclusion, sometimes by way of ridicule, scorn, hounding, ostracism, perhaps exile, this nevertheless has always seemed to me to represent the true responsibility of an artist. After all, how else did Ira Aldridge manage to get up on that stage and act every night, how else did Billie Holiday manage to walk the half dozen or so paces from the wings and stand before the microphone, how else did the great Paul Robeson simply manage to go through with another day? They did not need the missionaries (for the moment I shall call them critics) to guide them. Quite the reverse, history has shown us that it was the critics who were being led, guided like sullen children along a path they did not, they could not, understand. So why then, as I sat down to attempt to write *The Shelter*, the sudden problems? My word, my burden, 'responsibility'?

I thought long and hard that night and tried to grapple with the play, until the sun came up and the night was lost, and that page, if I remember correctly, was eventually covered by nothing more than a dozen or so lines of barely legible, over-corrected, circular ramblings, redundant jottings of something not yet understood. And for nearly three weeks time stood still as I tussled with the practical considerations of no longer being able to write. Untutored for any other profession I would eventually starve, I thought, but my piteous self-deception did not trouble me as much as the fact that I was clearly ready to capitulate and begin another project, and one not even related to theatre: television, prose, anything.

Then one evening I looked again to the postcard pinned up on the wall above my desk. I had bought it (in fact six copies) the previous year whilst recovering from England in France (although this particular hobby often feels like escaping Gillespie by putting on Satchmo: the swing is different but the beat remains the same). The postcard had immediately seized my eye, as would a garish street mural in Bath, for amongst the postcards of Van Gogh and Munch, Cézanne and Velásquez, the postcard was not simply exceptional in as much as it was a photograph, it also seemed to me to have its finger on the pulse of a difficult part of modern life, a part of life I wanted to know more about.

A white woman's face, probably that of a woman of thirty or thirty-five, who had probably just cried, or who would cry; and curled around her forehead, with just enough pressure to cause a line of folds in the skin above her eyes, were two black hands; obviously power and strength slept somewhere within them but at this moment they were infinitely gentle, describing with eight fingers that moment when a grip of iron weakens to a caress of love.

It had taken me only a few Parisian seconds to decide that the next play I would write would be about this postcard and would involve just one black man and one white woman. And now, as I faltered, I had to ask myself if I was frightened of the subject-matter? Was the responsibility of choosing to write about this postcard too great a burden for me to shoulder?

Somebody, a friend, a black woman, a journalist and politician, once told me, in fact threatened me with her truth, that until black writers stopped being obsessed by white women then black people would never achieve anything as a community, as a people, as a race. But, as I listened to her, I could not help recalling the stories of black men swinging from trees because some white woman had claimed (her husband having overslept that morning and not paid enough attention to her), that 'the nigger looked at her kinda funny.' I recalled Desdemona's father rejecting her:

"God be with you! I have done...
I am glad at soul I have no other child;"

and Othello's despair when he finally realizes the magnitude of his crime:

"I kiss'd thee ere I kill'd thee; no way but this,
Killing myself to die upon a kiss."

And I recalled also the hatred that the white press unleashed against Jack Johnson, the first black heavyweight champion, for having the audacity 'to parade' with a white woman. All my friend had done was merely to confirm what I knew all along: the story of the black man and the white woman in the Western world is bound together with the secure tape of a troubled history; and the relationship between the black man and the white woman has always provoked the greatest conflict, the most fear, the most loathing. For someone to suggest that black writers (or white writers for that matter) should flee from it is to suggest that we turn our backs on what is our arrogant but inevitable task; in other words to describe the world in which we live, as we see it, for those who also live in it, in order that they may see it clearer, and understand it better for themselves. This includes both black people and white people, especially the couple in the postcard who were probably too busy trying to survive from day to day to have the time or luxury to make a real sense of the lies and half-lies that threatened to consume their lives.

For over a year I had sat with my picture of the woman's face and the man's hands. I wanted them to stare at me, not me at them (for I knew I was not brave enough to endure such a prolonged two-way encounter), in the hope that I would one day, one night, willingly submit myself to a period of literary amnesia. But when I did try the pen rebelled, dried up, and the postcard remained an unresolved mystery. And, as I looked again at the card, I tried to piece together my thoughts. An explosive, perhaps the most explosive of all relationships, seldom written about, seldom explained, feared, observed, hated; did this place a greater responsibility upon me? Did this mean I had been struck dumb at the prospect of getting it wrong (whatever 'wrong' may mean)? As the hours turned over like the pages of a book, as yet unwritten, I wanted so much for this to be the solution to my hesitation. In fact I yearned for an end to it, not in truth so that there might be a new beginning, but, sadly, just so that there might be an end. The responsibility was too big, I would say, to myself only; and I would wait until I was more mature. Thinking coyly of the Aldridges, the Holidays, the Robesons, they too must know that the subject was too big, the responsibility too large, they would understand. And so, for what I thought might be the last time, I looked to the postcard but this time it was like looking in a mirror and suddenly realizing that you look like your father. A hand grabbed me and held me, and an unseen voice told me that I would never be able to run from it for the postcard was a part of me and if I did not acknowledge it I would be haunted, for the card had both fed and been feeding off my life. And true enough, like looking into my father's face, I clearly saw in it, perhaps for the first time, something that had made me what I was. I therefore turned back to my desk having learnt a little about self-deception and realizing now that the question of an additional responsibility was not the problem. The real problem was an age-old one, and one which could hardly lay claim to being particularly original. 'How should I write the play?' And, tackling the question involved declaring war on a word different from 'responsibility', but near cousin to it: the word 'expectation'.

The missionaries expect the natives to eagerly accept their religious beliefs and their moral strictures as the only ones available within which to think and act. They do not expect a native to first scale then challenge the pulpit, let alone become Pope; they expect mere imitation. Therefore the critic for the *Yorkshire Post* reviewed my first play, *Strange Fruit*, thus: 'Mr Phillips has pillaged the white man's theatre knowledgedly for a powerful, rangy, tragic play which is, ironically, about black men's roots.' And at that moment I stopped and thought about whether I should continue to write for the theatre, realizing then, at the start, that all that was expected of me, in order to elicit praise, was that I should ape this 'white man's theatre' and re-write versions of *Strange Fruit* in an ever increasingly bleached fashion. The word 'knowledgedly' may have been meant as praise but it was certainly not received as such; it was public acknowledgement that I was now a part of a club I did not wish to be part of: 'the white man's theatre' club. I did not, and still do not, recognize the validity of such an exclusive membership card, for the facts are clear and simple. In Africa I was not black. In Africa I was a writer. In Europe I am black. In Europe I am a black writer. If the missionaries wish to play the game along these lines then I do not wish to be an honorary white, and do the state some service, for that tough task-master, history, has shown us the folly of such deceit.

So the question of how to write this play involved not only the normal technical considerations but also those associated with being crudely pre-packaged as a particular sort of imitator. However, to have unpinned the postcard from the wall and written yet another 'knowledgable' domestic tragedy would have meant, as James Baldwin so eloquently put it, 'Making peace with my own mediocrity' and stepping into an area whose parameters are defined not by what one can do, but by what one perhaps ought to do. The end result of such a step for myself probably involves life membership of that most exclusive of clubs by taking what Langston Hughes called 'the unintentional bribe'. But as two plays now become three, and three might possibly become four, one is left wondering as to whether in time the carrot may be replaced by the stick?

Caryl Phillips
London, 1983

ACT ONE

CHARACTERS

HER: About 35. A country lady from somewhere between Bath and Bristol.

HIM: About 45. He looks a challenging man.

This act is set sometime towards the end of the eighteenth century, the age of the Augustans, of all that is rational and exact.

Note
The music for her song in Act One is Haydn Symphony No.39 in G. Minor (second movement), and this can also be used as incidental music at both the start and the end of Act One.

SCENE ONE

The lights come up on a stretch of white sand. On this beach are two sloping palms, some seaweed, some pieces of wood, a few coconuts, some masting, and some coconut shells.

The sun is high and we can hear the sea.

Downstage there is a woman lying on the sand. She is asleep, or unconscious, but clearly not dead for she stirs slightly. Then she is quiet again. She has on a tatty, long, dress but her legs are bare and she has on only the one shoe.

A man enters. He has on a large white cotton shirt, knee breeches, but no stockings or shoes. His hair is rough and full of sand and his face is slightly cut and scarred. Into the top of his breeches he has tucked a small knife. He carries a bundle of pieces of wood of different sizes which he piles down beside those that are already there. He looks at the woman and takes off his shirt. He places it over the woman to shield her from the sun. He moves offstage again.

After a few seconds the man comes back on with more wood. He goes across and stands over the woman as if checking to make sure that she is still breathing. She stirs and he drops back.

Overhead a gull cackles. The man looks up and accidentally drops the wood. He turns back to see the woman pulling herself up and looking at him.

HER: Do not touch me. I mean you no harm.
       [*She moves backwards, throwing his shirt off her. She holds on to the foot of a palm tree.*]
HIM: There is nothing to fear.
HER: Do not approach me.
HIM: I promise you, I have no desire to harm you.
       [*He carefully picks up his shirt and puts it on.*]

I sought to protect you from the heat of the sun with this, my shirt.
HER: You speak English?
HIM: I do. It is my only language.
> [*Pause.*]

HER: Is this your country?
HIM: Like you I was of England whose chalk-cliffed fringes we may never again set our eyes upon.
> [*Pause.*]

HER: Where are we?
HIM: I cannot be sure.
> [*Pause.*]

HER: Do not come any closer.
HIM: I bear you no malice.
HER: Remain where you are.
> [*Pause. She looks around.*]

Who are you?
HIM: My name or my position?
HER: What are you?
HIM: I am nobody to you.
> [*Pause.*]

I have things to do.
> [*He turns and goes offstage. She runs a nervous hand through her hair and tries to take stock of her surroundings. He comes back in with another bundle of wood and drops it.*]

HER: How do we come to be here? Are there no others?
HIM: The ship splintered and cast us both asunder.
HER: We two alone?
HIM: I assume the others to have perished.
> [*Pause.*]

It would appear our situation is the matter from which books are written, fortunes made.
> [*He continues to pile up the wood and shred the various materials into binding.*]

HER: You have markings of some sort upon your face.

[He reaches up and wipes away the dirt, etc.]

HIM: Bruising from the wreckage. I bled profusely.

[Pause.]

HER: Tell me truly how I come to find myself on these shores. I am near three decades adrift from childhood.

HIM: I discovered you clinging to a length of planking and I hauled you onto this sand.

HER: You rescued me?

HIM: It may be more accurate to intimate that I certainly prevented your drowning.

[Pause.]

At first I thought your death an inescapable certainty. For the last two days you have lain between heaven and earth.

HER: And what did you do with me?

HIM: Gave you water, what little fruit you could eat. I tried not to move your person beyond what was strictly necessary.

HER: You touched me?

HIM: I dragged you bodily from the ocean.

HER: I wish to sit upright.

[He moves towards her.]

I need no assistance.

[Pause.]

I have no recollection of your being aboard the ship. What was your position?

HIM: Merely a voyager.

HER: Of what status?

HIM: A common status.

[Pause. He continues binding the wood.]

HER: And what of our geography? You must have some notion of our position. Is this Africa?

HIM: If you look back to the hills... *[He points.]* You may have to stand to see them.

HER: I need not instruction in how to observe.

HIM: From their summit it is possible for one to traverse the whole island and beyond. There is nothing but sea in every direction.
HER: Then this is an island?
HIM: It is.
HER: The mist and cloud must obscure the horizon.
HIM: The days have been clear.
[*Pause.*]
HER: And what of the population of this so-called island?
HIM: We would appear to constitute the population.
HER: You are my sole companion?
HIM: I am.
HER: I do not believe you. Your understanding is weak.
HIM: It is based on exploration. Knowledge.
[*Pause.*]
HER: You masquerade as a gentleman. What are you?
HIM: A man. Gentle by nature.
HER: I have no desire to talk with you. I feel sure you have not within you the capacity for reason.

[*They stare at each other then he again begins to line up the wood into different lengths and bind it together. She pretends to be concerned with her dress and wiping clean her bruises and the dirt from off her face. She tries to untangle her hair. He wipes his brow then goes for more wood. He comes back and once again begins the whole process of binding and sorting.*]

Do you not feel ashamed to look at me in that manner?
HIM: I know not what manner it is you speak of.
HER: That unclean manner.
HIM: I have not looked upon you in any manner, clean or unclean. I am occupied.
HER: To what possible end?
HIM: Constructing an ungainly but secure refuge from wrappings of cloth and strands of foliage.

HER: I trust you are not thinking I might be encouraged to enter into it with something such as yourself.
HIM: I understand.
HER: You must possess fanciful notions of my character.
HIM: Our acquaintance has been too brief for such speculation.
HER: A theatrical thing such as yourself conversing with ceremony?
HIM: I am not offended that you do not wish to share my island chambers.
HER: It would be akin to breaking bread with the devil.
   [*Pause.*]
HIM: I know not why it is you wish to fight with me.
   [*Pause. He continues with what he was doing.*]
HER: Why do you choose to construct a dwelling?
HIM: To avoid death from the naked heat of the sun and its resultant giddiness. And, if there be wild animals loose on the island we must have need of some defences to preserve our lives.
HER: Wild animals?
HIM: Hypothesis is near cousin to safety with knowledge as scant as our own.
HER: There are no wild animals. Either your imagination is defective or your exploration superficial.
   [*He carries on with what he is doing and again he goes off for more wood. He brings it back on and gets to the next stage in the construction of his shelter. She 'bravely' stands and looks about herself. She takes off her one shoe and takes something out of it. She wipes it clean on her sleeve and puts it back on. She begins to take an interest in what he is doing but she does not want him to see she is interested.*]
   Is it your idleness of race prevents your building a boat?
   [*Pause. He ignores her.*]

And tell me, are you truly bereft of human faculties?
HIM: I am not possessed of the skills necessary to construct a boat.

[*Pause. She walks about a little.*]

HER: I shall not be staying here. We cannot be far from the African mainland and we can sail there swiftly.
HIM: Have you some knowledge of which direction to set sail?
HER: It is quite straightforward. You will read the stars.
HIM: It is the middle of the afternoon.
HER: You overestimate your cleverness, ape.

[*Pause.*]

HIM: I shall continue in the construction of quarters, for night will be upon us sooner than we may imagine.
HER: And tomorrow?
HIM: I shall arise and approach the day with both care and caution.
HER: No, you will build a boat.
HIM: And what of the weather? We two alone survive a storm that sank an ocean-going vessel.
HER: The storm has blown over.
HIM: But there will be others to follow. And what of supplies? Fresh water? Food-stocks?
HER: We shall manage.

[*Pause. He picks up two of the coconut shells.*]

HIM: I have found inland a freshwater stream. Do you wish to explore?
HER: I shall go nowhere, heathen.

[*He goes off and she waits a moment before coming over and looking at the wood and binding, etc. She picks up a stick but throws it down in disgust. She turns and looks out to sea. He comes back in, carrying more binding.*]

HIM: I have noticed you have on only the one shoe.
HER: It is no concern of yours.
HIM: Why not remove it and walk barefoot in comfort?

HER: I was not born of savage stock.
   [*Pause. She looks at him but he continues to work.*]
HIM: What might a lady such as yourself be doing aboard the *St. Christopher*?
HER: Nothing that would concern something of your kind.
HIM: Perhaps not.
   [*Pause.*]
   I assume your husband to be a merchant on the coast.
HER: He will certainly set sail to search me out.
HIM: Then it would appear there is no reason for us to risk our lives upon uncharted seas.
HER: You will construct a boat.
HIM: But there is much to eat. We might cook on alternate days.
HER: Cook?
HIM: Seagulls' eggs, fish, crab, fruit.
HER: Impudent.
   [*Pause. She turns away from him. He starts to dig out the sand so that he can erect the walls.*]
   I command you to build me a means of leaving these shores.
HIM: There is nothing here to make you important to me, nothing that might induce me to obey the harshness of your voice.
   [*Pause.*]
HER: I know you as an escaped slave, do I not?
   [*He laughs.*]
HIM: A slave, lady? Where are my chains? Where is my master? Are you my mistress?
   [*Pause. He continues to laugh.*]
   How am I a slave?
HER: Nigger.
HIM: Lady, I am a free man in as much as any man is able to be free. I belong to nobody.
HER: You remain here out of fear of what might befall you if you leave, slave.

HIM: I remain because I choose to remain.
[*He carries on building and she looks at the sea.*]
HER: Do you have a name, slave?
HIM: They tell me it is Thomas Samuels.
HER: Who are 'they'?
HIM: Your family, lady.
HER: You do not know of my family.
HIM: And you do not know of mine, lady.
HER: Your family attachments are those of a dog.
[*Pause.*]
You may call me Mrs. Darnley or Ma'am. I am not accustomed to being addressed as 'lady'.
[*He laughs.*]
I find your laughter primitive.
[*Pause.*]
Your lips are uncommonly thick. Can you say, 'Ma'am'?
HIM: Ma'am.
HER: You surprise me.
[*Pause.*]
If we must pass some minutes here it is only Christian to name the island.
[*Pause.*]
'Palm Tree Island' would seem both accurate and relevant.
HIM: I have already named it, 'The Island'.
HER: 'The Island'? You mean to give it no name at all?
HIM: It is accurate. It betrays nothing.
[*She laughs.*]
HER: It is stupid. Uncivilized.
[*Pause.*]
When you have completed your games you will light a fire to attract the attention of passing ships.
HIM: It would involve one of us living on top of the hill to keep it ablaze, for it is the only true vantage point.
HER: Then you must live there.

[*He ignores her and strains to support and put up some of the shelter. He does so, making a very flimsy hut. He stands back from it, having tossed the knife down by the excess binding.*]

It is truly grotesque. I would expect little more from you.

[*He picks up a bit of stick and begins to draw idly in the sand.*]

[*looking at the shelter*] I quite fail to see the other room.

[*He looks angrily at her.*]

My sleeping quarters.

HIM: You sleep where you stand.

HER: You need a stiff beating, Samuels. You have no manners in the presence of a lady.

HIM: It matters little to me be you a lady or a vagabond.

HER: And you claim you are free, that you have nothing to fear from the company of other men.

HIM: I have much to fear in any man's presence but it is not the chains that I dread, it is the manner of thought that flashes between a man's clapping eyes on me and the opening of his mouth. It is not his touch but the hesitation before his touch. In England I was nothing, a man of colour labouring for a nobleman, born into servitude, for England is too perfumed a country to soil her own people with the word slavery.

[*Pause.*]

But some masters die and mine did oblige.

[*Pause.*]

And what in this Africa that we set sail for? Will you and your husband try and buy this freeman as your slave?

[*Pause.*]

Though I be no man's slave, lady, I remain a slave to the state of your world but I fear you not. I may yet find a corner of this earth where you do not exist.

[*She walks away from him.*]

The Shelter

HER: Construct a boat and take me but a part of the way. You may cut me loose in a smaller boat and thereafter roam where you will.

> [*Pause.*]

I have money. I will pay you.

> [*She reaches down into the pockets of her dress and pulls loose a couple of coins. He begins to draw in the sand.*]

HIM: I do not wish to leave our island.

HER: I am no part of it. Is there no talking to you?

HIM: I know not how to construct a boat.

> [*Pause.*]

And I see not a wedding ring upon your finger.

> [*She stares at him for a long while then she runs and picks up the knife, which is on the sand. She turns to face him.*]

HER: You will build a boat and take me away.

HIM: Woman, your words betray foolishness.

HER: No, slave. I am sincere in my convictions. Do not come any closer.

HIM: And to where shall we sail?

HER: Navigation is a skill more becoming a man.

HIM: And am I now a man?

> [*Pause.*]

Lady, I do not see your overseer. Does a knife alone now give you authority over me?

> [*He takes a step towards her.*]

HER: Do not come any closer or I shall do it.

HIM: Do what, lady?

> [*He takes the knife from her.*]

We left behind such behaviour when I hauled you ashore.

HER: I cannot stay here with an ape.

> [*Pause.*]

HIM: Then one of us must leave.

HER: Ape.

[*Pause.*]

HIM: Your ignorance clings to you like sand to a moist limb.
> [*They stare at each other; overhead a gull cackles. The sea is heard sliding up the beach and then it is quiet. He moves away from her and looks out to sea. She stares at him.*]

SCENE TWO

Only a few moments have passed. She is sitting now. He looks at the shelter then pushes at it and knocks it over. He stares at her, wanting to see her response. She drops her eyes and he goes offstage.

At first she does nothing but look out to sea. However, after a while she begins to worry if he is going to come back. She stands and moves nervously to where he went off then she comes back and looks at the broken shelter.

Then she hears him and it startles her. She manages to sit down before he appears. He has his arms full of palm leaves. He throws them down and begins to arrange them. They say nothing to each other.

HER: You have been quite some time.
> [*Pause. He ignores her.*]

I dislike being left alone. Desertion is not mannerly.
> [*He starts to work, unstripping some of the binding and reworking some of the rest. She watches him.*]

Tell me, why destroy your own construction? It seems uncommonly self-defeating.
> [*Pause.*]

I can only assume maritime matters are under way.

HIM: Perhaps you have spoken sufficiently as it is.

HER: I am not in need of your help in the conducting of my conversational affairs.

[*Pause.*]

I should like to know if you are engaged in the process of building a vessel.

HIM: I am.

HER: And of what variety is this vessel?

HIM: A raft. It is the best I can do.

[*She laughs.*]

HER: You do not surprise me.

[*Pause. He ignores her and continues working.*]

I have no intention of reinforcing your own position, do you understand?

[*Pause.*]

Merely remember you are in the presence of a lady who has never before left England.

HIM: It would seem to matter not where you people go. Your behaviour remains much the same.

[*He draws a line in the sand with a piece of stick.*]

I would rather you remained on the further side of this line.

HER: And what is to happen if I venture to cross your line?

HIM: Perhaps nothing.

HER: You make little sense. You continue to converse as a child.

HIM: And you as someone who will continue to grow in confidence and ignorance.

[*Pause. She stands.*]

HER: I intend to cross your line. Circumstances cannot alter the clarity of the situation.

[*He says nothing so she crosses the line.*]

There. I have crossed it. What are your intentions?

HIM: They are simple. Upon the completion of this raft I shall take my departure.

HER: And what of me?
HIM: There is fresh water and food. You will survive.
HER: I must accompany you. To abandon me would be murder.
HIM: Lady, you belittle me.
HER: And you me with the staleness of your black mind.
  [*Pause.*]
HIM: Your husband will find you.
HER: My husband is dead. A squire, thirty years older than I.
  [*Pause.*]
  I am a widow going to the coast in the hope of attracting a good match amongst the merchants there.
  [*Pause.*]
  I am not ashamed. My future husband will reward you handsomely.
HIM: Your future husband will be a trifle deaf, his ears affected by the bloodied screams of dying Africans. He will not know how to reward such as I.
HER: I will instruct him to let you have whatever it is you desire.
  [*He begins to laugh. She looks angrily to him.*]
  Your fetid smell offends me.
  [*He continues to laugh until he is able to speak.*]
HIM: I was born near 200 years ago in a small village in my native Africa.
  [*Pause.*]
HER: Your statement lacks any proportion. It is that of a nigger.
HIM: A village so small that I cannot remember the name of it... and your father came and set fire to the hut of my family, raped my mother and killed my own aged father, but he did not kill me for I was young and strong. He beat me till I bled unconscious on the ground. He chained together my hands and my legs, then he fired an iron rod and branded my skin as

easily as a hot knife finds its way through a waxen candle. The smell jolted my person to consciousness.

[*Pause.*]

Then he placed me in a large ship with others of my village and he took me to a country where he punished me if I spoke my own language, to a country where he whipped me if I worshipped my own Gods, and in their place he gave me the cold European tongue I now speak and the long-haired white man I am supposed to worship.

[*Pause.*]

When I had my children your father took them from me as he took the grain that I had harvested, the cane that I cut, the cotton that I picked, and he still takes them from me.

[*Pause.*]

I see your father in the face of every white man I discern, and I do not want your future husband to reward me for he has not the money to repay the debt.

HER: My father was a good man. He kept no niggers.

[*He laughs.*]

HIM: I am 200 years old now, and getting older. I wonder when you will die and we can begin anew?

HER: Do not threaten me.

HIM: Can you learn to perceive again? Witness the whole red-stained world?

HER: I can see perfectly.

HIM: And what do you see?

HER: I see you. The awful thickness of your lips. Your tumid nostrils, your teeth like small tusks, your eyes round and mis-shapened like blackened farthings, your head covered in a bestial fleece. I see that somebody has evidently caused you a great hurt and you still smart with the pain; you still try to achieve a primitive revenge.

HIM: I hurt for whosoever it was etched the first cut he has

Act One

never troubled to dress the wound properly. And every time I renew the dressing he comes and again he tears it off.

HER: I find your plea for pity sickening. Like all slaves you merely beg.

HIM: I beg nothing from you.

> [*Pause. He turns away from her.*]

The light fails quickly.

> [*Pause.*]

And we shall be in need of more wood for the fire.

> [*She says nothing and he goes off. But he accidentally leaves behind the knife. She bends down and picks it up. Then she tosses it back down and waits... He comes back in and starts to construct a fire. He feels in his waistband for the knife then realizes he has left it behind. He looks down and he picks it up. She looks away. He starts to cut up the bits of wood.*]

Tell me, why could you not find yourself a match in England?

HER: It is not that simple. I have a position to maintain.

HIM: Order and degree.

HER: You may mock but it keeps our people above the animal, gives us a purpose, and it is what is right in God's name.

HIM: It is you who are chained.

> [*Pause.*]

Destined to echo the awful piety of a previous people.

HER: And what would you suggest?

HIM: Nothing. I know only that England has exchanged her aristocracy for this new steam age, and her|men of colour will never be happy, will never dream without the sun kissing their faces, till the cold morning strikes them alive. And those amongst us, like you, who dare, must leave. That is all I know. Nothing. There is no suggestion.

> [*Pause.*]

The Shelter

HER: There must have been some desirable women of your kind in England.

HIM: A few, but they too had positions to maintain. In the kitchens of your family.

HER: And what of the lower English women? I hear that...

HIM: You see, I never before felt able to associate with someone who, without the discipline of forethought, merely realized of me as a nigger, or as a slave, or as one who might take nourishment from eating the flesh of my fellow human beings. I was always inclined towards the notion that I would, perhaps against my will, kill them.

> [*He stoops and strikes the knife against the stone. After a few attempts it catches fire on the dry sticks and moss, etc. He starts to blow on the fire to encourage it to flare up.*]

There. It is alight.

HER: You have some practical skills.

> [*Pause. He says nothing.*]

It seems we have little choice but to pass this one night here.

HIM: We have everything we need.

> [*He tucks the knife into his belt.*]

I shall gather more wood.

> [*He moves to go off.*]

HER: No.

> [*He stops and turns to face her.*]

The noises of the day seem magnified by night.

> [*Pause. He says nothing.*]

If you wish to kill me, do so now and not whilst I sleep.

> [*Pause.*]

HIM: I shall not be long.

> [*She turns away and he throws down his knife without her seeing. Then he moves off quickly. She wanders nervously and sings quietly to herself. After a few minutes she begins to wonder where he is.*]

HER: [*singing*]
As it came on a bright day our Lord asked his mother,
If he might wander free, wander free, on the hill.
Up and down our sweet Lord ran till three poor young men,
Said to him come with us, come with us, you will see.

> [*She moves to where he has gone off and comes back to the fire where she sees the knife, which she picks up. She hovers over the fire, her face glowing in the light. Gradually the silence of the night and the sound of the waves begin to take over. She is frightened and convinced that he has deserted her. She begins to sing again to keep herself company. Then out of the darkness he comes back.*]

I was sure of your desertion.

HIM: I omitted to take my knife.

> [*He takes it from her and walks down past her to the edge of the sea.*]

HER: I must admit to being fearful of the dark.

HIM: You were singing.

HER: It is no concern of yours.

HIM: It was possessed of a fine melody.

> [*Pause.*]

HER: Are you not going for more wood?

HIM: I may manage with what I have.

> [*We hear the sea as they both wait in silence. Almost without knowing it she begins to sing to herself again.*]

HER: [*singing*]
Over fields ran he three poor men a chasing,
But a sight of such wealth, of such wealth, brought him to his knee.
And fetched home Mary mild her child who suffered,
Then she took him into her arms, in her arms, and affection showered she.

> [*He turns around and she stops abruptly.*]

HIM: You sing well.
HER: I offer it more as a prayer than as a form of entertainment. Something to help pass the night.
HIM: [*quietly, as he moves away from her*] And the next day, and the night, and the day after that.
    [*Pause. The noise of the sea grows angrier.*]
HER: Did you choose to speak?
HIM: Only if you were listening, lady. Only if you chose to listen.

ACT TWO

CHARACTERS

IRENE

LOUIS

This act is set in the bar of a pub in Ladbroke Grove, London, some time in the 1950s.

Act Two

We are in a grimy Ladbroke Grove pub. It is mid-evening in mid-week and there are very few people in the bar.

IRENE: *Close on thirty-five. She sits at a round, slightly unbalanced table by herself. She listens to the crackly jukebox as one fifties ballad finishes and the machinery heaves itself into another well-worn period tune. She is dressed in a skirt and top. She still has on a thin jacket, which we assume is too flimsy for the cold January weather outside. She clings to it and sips at her half pint of light ale. Her fingers and face are clean though they look grubby and well-worn. Her face is pleasant, though tired, as she begins to slide into premature middle age. She is agitated and anxious.*

Enter LOUIS: *As if straight from work in his donkey jacket and working trousers and boots. He looks at* IRENE *for a moment then comes over, pint in hand, and stands over her. We see that his hands are chafed and dirty. He too looks tired.*

IRENE *looks up at* LOUIS, *then away from him, pretending to listen to the music, which eventually finishes.*

Pause.

LÓUIS: I don't want to disturb you. I just want to sit down and take a quiet drink.
    [IRENE *looks up at* LOUIS *then turns away.*]
IRENE: I don't mind.
LOUIS: I can stand if you like but I'm tired out and I would quite like a seat.
    [*Pause.*]
    All right, then?
    [IRENE *says nothing.* LOUIS *sits down.*]
    I'm sorry.
IRENE: What for?
LOUIS: Nudging your train of thought onto a different track. Derailing it. A little mix-up at the junctions.
    [*Pause.*]

| | I work on the railways.
| | [*Pause.*]
| | But I don't speak like this all the time.
| IRENE: | I don't think anybody could. Too much of a strain.
| LOUIS: | True.
| | [*Pause.*]
| | But I thought you might like to know in case you're maybe thinking it's a little madness that's licking me down.
| IRENE: | No, I don't think you're mad.
| LOUIS: | No? I'm glad. For all I want to do in truth is to sit down and take a quiet drink and be on my way.
| | [IRENE *looks sharply at him.*]
| | Out into the cold and foggy London streets where the light spills carelessly from lamp to tramp.
| IRENE: | Where?
| LOUIS: | And from around the lazy corner the sharp leathery clicking of the dull man's shoes echoes in the chilly fifties air. Tonight, dark starry night, the dusky stranger plunges deeper and deeper into the moonlit abyss of hell.
| IRENE: | You sound like a loony even if you're not one.
| LOUIS: | Loony, lunatic, lunar, moon, moonlit. We're on the same wavelength.
| IRENE: | We are?
| | [*Pause.*]
| LOUIS: | They used to tell me I was a poet. At school.
| IRENE: | You work on the railways.
| LOUIS: | Things are hard at the moment.
| | [*Pause.*]
| | We go in a barber shop and they tell us they don't know how to cut a coloured man's hair rather than they don't want to cut a coloured man's hair. I can't even get a haircut. That's how bad things are. And getting worse.
| IRENE: | Things haven't been much different for some of us. One frigging crisis after another and all for what?

LOUIS: You know the saying, 'If things are bad for the populus then they are impossible for the poet'?
IRENE: I never did read much.
LOUIS: I just made it up.
IRENE: Well then how am I supposed to have heard it before?
LOUIS: I don't know. It's just a way of saying something.
> [*Pause.*]
> Sorry. I didn't want to disturb you.
IRENE: That's all right.
> [*Pause.*]
> You're not disturbing me.
> [*Pause.*]
> Am I disturbing you?
LOUIS: Even when the small child peers at the humming bird from behind a low bush he still disturbs the bird for the bird knows.
> [*Pause.*]
> Tell the lone shark that he must come to a party up in the hills with the deer and the wild pig and the fowl, and play amongst the hibiscus with the monkey. Tell him so and see what happens. The shock of it will kill him. He can't last. Kill him dead, pow, dead like a piece of driftwood washed up on a lazy beach at sunset.
> [*Pause.*]
> Dead like a bird that flies too close to the sun. Pow!
> [*Pause.*]
> Dead like an Englishman on a summer's day. Dead.
> [*Pause.*]
> Dead.
IRENE: Dead?
LOUIS: Dead.
IRENE: You must have been drinking. Before you came in here.
LOUIS: Where?
IRENE: 'Cross and Anchor' for instance.
LOUIS: 'Cross and Anchor'?

IRENE: You know the 'Cross and Anchor'. Further up the Grove. Paddy Sullivan's place. Big place. Used to be nice. When it first opened.
  [*Pause.*]
  You've heard of Paddy Sullivan. Drunk the Holyhead to Dublin ferry dry Christmas '53, '54 and '55, before they banned him. Rumour has it they paid him off if he wouldn't travel on it again, which is how he made it from navvy to landlord without so much as a bat of an eyelid. Others say the I.R.A. gave him some money for killing a man. Loyalist man it must have been.
  [*Pause.*]
  Bit fanciful that one, even for these parts.
  [*Pause.*]
  The old man, Jack, he was from Ireland, Dublin proper. Used to piss it up with Paddy Sullivan every night towards the end till I told him where to get off.
LOUIS: To get off?
IRENE: You know, piss off, on his bike. Take a long walk off a short pier.
LOUIS: I see now.
IRENE: He finally got the message. Eight years of rubbish.
  [*Pause.*]
  First year was the best year. Visiting Mum on a Sunday.
  [*Pause.*]
LOUIS: There are too many coloured men in this country at one time. And the children we left behind with the women, they are going to end up more women than men. Just pretty-waisted men. Sexy prisoners to England, visiting Mum on a Sunday.
  [*He laughs, then stops. Pause.*]
  But maybe they're soon going to have to start sending us the food parcels and the clothes We, the pioneers, to make life bearable for them. Slaves.
  [IRENE *reaches across and puts her hand on his.*]

Act Two

IRENE: You're shivering. Are you cold?
LOUIS: Have you ever felt a snowflake sting?
IRENE: Have you just come in here for a warm or do you want another drink?
LOUIS: No, no, no...
> [*Pause.*]

I would like another drink please.
IRENE: Another pint then, Casey Jones.
LOUIS: Casey who?
IRENE: Another pint?
LOUIS: My name is not Casey.
IRENE: Sorry.
> [*She stands.*]

Guinness?
> [*He looks at her and nods. She moves off.* LOUIS *begins to hum along nervously with the song on the jukebox and he looks anxiously around. He takes out a pack of ten cigarettes and taps them on the side of the table to the beat.* IRENE *comes back with a pint of Guinness and a bottle of light ale for herself. She sets them down on the table and sits.*]

Do you need a match because I haven't got one.
> [LOUIS *pushes the cigarettes back into his pocket.*]

LOUIS: I can't afford it. I'm saving up for the future.
> [*Pause.*]

IRENE: Do you like this music?
LOUIS: Why?
IRENE: I know you like music.
LOUIS: I suppose so. There's nothing wrong with a nice steady rhythm. A steady beat.
> [*Pause.*]

A nice string band working up a mood or a pan ringing out in the still afternoon air when the school children begin to walk by the side of the road on their way home, their books on top of their heads to shield them from the sun. That's how I remember music.

[*Pause.*]
Stories keep breaking up inside me.
IRENE: What stories?
LOUIS: I'm sorry. I can't say everything I want to say. It's all messed up now.
IRENE: I was thinking of playing the jukebox if you'll lend us a tanner.
LOUIS: Sure, sure.
[*He roots around in his pocket for one.*]
IRENE: It's three for sixpence. You can have a choice too.
LOUIS: No, I trust you. You make the choice.
IRENE: If you're sure you trust me.
LOUIS: I'm going to have to trust you for I don't know the music too good.
IRENE: But do you trust me?
LOUIS: What?
[*Pause.* IRENE *gets up and goes to the jukebox.*]
IRENE: Do you want something special?
LOUIS: If you like.
IRENE: What?
LOUIS: Spiritual.
IRENE: Hymns?
LOUIS: I don't believe in God any more. I'm not a child any more.
IRENE: That's not right. You should have told me.
[*She chooses the music and sits. It starts up again.*]
But it's up to you, I suppose. I sometimes wonder myself.
LOUIS: There's nothing wrong with wondering. Unless you start to do too much of it.
[*Pause.*]
IRENE: Are you really a poet? I mean, have you ever really thought seriously about writing some of your stuff down?
[*Pause.*]
I can help, you know.

LOUIS: How?
IRENE: I can write letters, can't I? I can ring people up and tell them about you.
LOUIS: My mother said I had good hair and thin lips. In time I could be somebody. Back home. If I followed the true path of the Lord and righteousness. A poet even, but you're right. I'm just talking foolishness. Poetry and that sort of thing is for rich white people.
   [*Pause.*]
   Good hair and thin lips.
IRENE: You look all right to me as you are.
LOUIS: I cut cane to start with.
   [*Pause.*]
   My father said as long as the sun shines and the night falls, as long as the soil is rich and the rain hard and sharp, a man can cut cane. Now all that can happen and if a man can't think of a word of poetry to say he's going to stand and look down as his trousers ease their way over his shrinking waist, then his hips, then slither down his backside and leave the man high and dry and looking a damn fool.
   [*Pause.*]
   My father had some funny ways of putting things but he was always a truthful man, always told it like it was even when he knew it was going to hurt.
   [*Pause.*]
   Like when he told me, a ten-year-old boy, that coloured men shouldn't think too much.
   [*Pause.*]
IRENE: Jack used to work in books, you know.
LOUIS: Books, newspapers, pamphlets, leaflets, I like them all. England is good for that. I can't beat her there.
   [*Pause.*]
   But it's not like what they said it would be. People are bad here. Bad, bad.
IRENE: Not everybody.

LOUIS: Everybody.
IRENE: That's not fair.
LOUIS: Yes everybody...
IRENE: But you can't,..
LOUIS: What about the books?
[*Pause.*]
IRENE: I was going to tell you.
[*Pause.*]
The thing was, the only kind of books I ever saw him with had pictures of naked women in them. Used to leave the filth around the house for anyone to see. Got so as I couldn't even ask a friend around in case one was under a cushion or in the bog.
LOUIS: It's only that he used to read?
IRENE: He was a dealer in the stuff. Porn. Hard porn.
LOUIS: He was older than you?
IRENE: Still is. Eight years. Married him when I was nineteen. He was twenty-seven then but he had a decent job at least. Joiner for a firm building a range of flats down Wandsworth way. It was great then. Visiting Mum on a Sunday.
[*Pause.*]
After work he'd come home, have a bath, then we'd go out clubbing it or pubbing it. Somewhere different every night, loads to spend, and end up pissed by midnight then back home slowly, to avoid the coppers. He was great then, in the first year. But then the job finished and he started to get into some dodgy jobs and the money stopped and that's when the books started. I'm boring, aren't I?
[*Pause.*]
I kicked him out like I told you I did. He didn't leave me.
LOUIS: Kicked him out?
IRENE: Told him to leave, to go, to move on.

Act Two

LOUIS: Which is what I did.
IRENE: No you didn't. I didn't ask you to...
LOUIS: Flee. Flee beauty like him.
IRENE: So you think I'm beautiful then, do you? Is that what you're trying to say?
LOUIS: You're like the island. You're a woman.
IRENE: What's that supposed to mean?
LOUIS: All islands are women. Except England. England is so hard she must be a man.
IRENE: Is it like in Africa over there? You know. The films.
>   [*Pause.*]
>
>   Humphrey Bogart. Katharine Hepburn. *The African Queen.*
>
>   [*Pause.*]
>
>   I just wondered.

LOUIS: I don't have anything to do with those people. I don't eat bananas on the top deck of a double-decker bus, and I don't walk around with my head in a damn book and tell all the girls my name is 'Prince' this, or 'Duke' the other.
IRENE: I know you don't.
LOUIS: Some of those African people make me sick.
>   [*Pause.*]
>
>   I'm a British subject.

IRENE: Object, isn't it?
>   [*Pause.*]

LOUIS: I'm a British object.
IRENE: Watching the smoke curl aimlessly across a grey skyline...
LOUIS: Watching the smoke curl aimlessly across a grey skyline...
IRENE: Feeling the cold bitter air snapping into my sun-kissed face...
LOUIS: Feeling the cold bitter air snapping into my sun-kissed face...

IRENE: Dreaming of home.
LOUIS: Dreaming of home.
   [*Pause.*]
IRENE: I like you Louis because you're not worn out even though you keep saying you are.
   [*Pause.*]
   If things were different then they'd be different and everything would be okay.
LOUIS: Maybe.
   [*Pause.*]
   There's more now. I thought of it today. Shunting.
IRENE: What?
LOUIS: Shunting. The Liverpool train into the depot. I was shunting at the time when I thought of it.
IRENE: I'm glad. I thought it was a dirty word for a minute. He went a bit that way when he started on the books. Used to try words out on me.
   [*Pause.*]
   At first I used to blush and cry sometimes. Then I stopped pretending I'd never heard them before and I started to repeat them back to him. Made him so mad he started to hit me then. Never a punch that might leave a mark, always a slap, sting rather than bruise. Always room for saying I'm sorry with a slap but not with a punch: a punch is too definite.
   [*Pause.*]
   Jesus Christ, he used to make a sound when he got drunk though. Like a dog when you keep standing on its tail all the time. I couldn't stand him or his noises. I married a man and ended up with a pig. Till I met you.
   [*Pause.*]
   I'd never seen a man cry till I met you.
LOUIS: Whilst I was shunting.
IRENE: I know. I haven't forgotten. Sorry.
   [*Pause.*]

Act Two

It's over a year now since I told him to go, isn't it? Fourteen months to be exact. He'll be thirty-five in the springtime. He called it April. I like calling it the springtime.

LOUIS: I know you do.
[*Pause.*]
My woman's smile is like a jagged knife.

IRENE: Is this it, then? The shunting poem. Can you shunt to it?
[*She laughs.*]

LOUIS: It cuts deep, bleeds ugly, drains life
From a man like me, born to be free
And live in the shadow of a hot, deep sea.
[*Pause.*]

IRENE: I don't get what you're trying to say.

LOUIS: My woman's touch is like a hunk of stone
It wounds and shivers and chills you to the bone
Her face, I loathe, her manners I hate,
And she thinks she can trap me with little grey bait.
[*Pause.*]

IRENE: I haven't done anything on purpose, Louis. It can still work out any way you want it to.
[*Pause.*]
Don't expect me to beg.

LOUIS: High above the fields, and just a little below the clouds,
The wind whispers through the trees, ignoring the clouds,
Out yonder floats a spot, like a thin black slither,
This cruel boat taking people, my people, to where they will shiver; wither and die.
[*Pause.*]

IRENE: All you have to say is that you don't regret anything. That's all I really want you to say.

LOUIS: Maybe I could turn it into a calypso and make some money that way, make my English fortune.

> [*As he begins to go through the last poem again, this time singing it to a calypso beat,* IRENE *tries to speak to him over the noise.*]

IRENE: I didn't expect to see you in here. I was just lonely. I just wanted a quiet drink.

> [*He comes to the end of the poem and repeats the last line.*]

LOUIS: Shiver, wither and die.

> [*Pause.*]

Shiver, wither and die. It doesn't seem to go in. More like a hymn ending.

IRENE: We can make it work but we just have to try harder than the others.

> [*Pause.*]

You said that, didn't you?

LOUIS: Maybe one of the other ones will fit better to the calypso beat.

IRENE: But I don't want to hear any of them any more.

LOUIS: So what happen? You don't like my poetry?

IRENE: People are starting to look at us.

LOUIS: People look at us anyway, Irene. Stare at us, for over a year now, like they're thinking they should be fucking, not out shopping for furniture, or at the pictures enjoying themselves, or on a bus going home, or having a drink, they think we should be fucking.

> [*He slaps the table.*]

They should be fucking.

> [*He slaps the table.*]

They should be fucking.

> [*He slaps the table.*]

They should be fucking.

IRENE: Louis, please, people are watching.

> [LOUIS *gets up and starts to fumble with his trousers.*]

LOUIS: We should be fucking, you and I, West Indian man and English woman.

Act Two

IRENE: For God's sake, Louis, sit down.
> [*She pushes him down into his seat.*]

Don't behave like that. Don't let them get to you like that.

LOUIS: But don't you see how they look, hoping we won't do anything human like laugh, or cry, or kiss.

IRENE: Please.

LOUIS: Kiss me.
> [*She moves to do so.*]

I don't mean on the cheek either. I mean properly. Like you mean it in truth.

IRENE: I do.

LOUIS: Well, if you mean it just kiss me full and let them watch.
> [IRENE *leans forward and they kiss. They hold for a moment then break.*]

IRENE: I don't care about them.

LOUIS: Are they still watching?

IRENE: Yes.
> [*Pause.*]

We'll never be able to come in here for a drink again but I don't mind.

LOUIS: A drink?

IRENE: I said I didn't mind. I don't.

LOUIS: A man can go anywhere in this country for a drink, so they tell us. It's a free country so come and take a drink where you like, brother, so long as you don't fall in love with any of our women. Fuck them, in private, by all means, but don't make them feel happy. Just make them feel grateful then leave them and take a drink where you like.

IRENE: Why are you going on like this?

LOUIS: So, we can drink someplace else.

IRENE: I know.

LOUIS: Do you want to continue to care in public?

IRENE: I don't know what you are talking about, Louis. All I know is I felt safe in here. I felt safe in here with you too.

LOUIS: Safe?

IRENE: Safe. But you don't care about me any more so why pretend you do? After a year you just disappear into the middle of the night.
> [*Pause.*]
>
> Doesn't it matter to you how I feel?

LOUIS: A man once warned me that when I get to England not to get involved with any of the white women for you can't take them back home with you for as soon as they set foot on the island they're going to start crying out for a hand-maiden and a butler and a maid, and how the hell can a cane-cutter afford such things?

IRENE: Don't talk stupid, Louis.

LOUIS: And the man who told me this went on and told me that women are just like a bowl of exotic fruit, and he likes to take a bite from them all, taste them a little, but he doesn't like to linger too long for when you get through to the core they are just like all fruit: hard, stony and bitter.

IRENE: I don't want to know those things...

LOUIS: And the man who told me this was my wife's father.
> [*Pause.*]
>
> Pushed his finger up into my face the night before I left and warned me that when I get to England not to get involved with any of the white women for you can't take them back home with you.

IRENE: He was just trying to put you off.

LOUIS: He didn't have to. I'd already made up my mind I wanted nothing to do with you.

IRENE: But you didn't know me.

LOUIS: White women.
> [*Pause.*]
>
> I was going to work, save, and send for my wife when

the time came, when I could feel proud enough to support her in a better style of life than she was accustomed to back home.

IRENE: But you said she went off with a fisherman.

LOUIS: She probably felt safe with him.
[*Pause.*]
First time I ever saw a white woman in England I knew I wanted one. Not necessarily to keep but so I could keep it if I wanted to.

IRENE: You told me this.

LOUIS: I'm not talking about you, though. I'm talking about before I met you. When I first came here.

IRENE: I don't know what to think any more.

LOUIS: But it's how it was. I wanted one. Like a child wants the latest toy. But it's not the child's life it ruins but the father's pocket.
[*Pause.*]
The father can always get a new pair of pants.
[*Pause. The music stops.* IRENE *reaches across and takes his hand.*]

IRENE: You look frightened, Louis.

LOUIS: I don't look like nothing. Frightened is too definite. I look like nothing.

IRENE: The music has stopped.

LOUIS: If you want an all-year round suntan for your children then marry to a coloured man. You can always call the child medium-rare.
[*Pause.* IRENE *stares at him. Then she stands. He reaches down into his pockets and pushes sixpence across the table to her. She touches his hand as she takes up the money. He notices but says nothing. She puts the money in the jukebox.*]

IRENE: There's not much we haven't played.
[*She begins to punch out her choices. Then she starts to sing to the song.*]

LOUIS: Over two years in this place now and I still feel like a

sparrow not an eagle.
>[IRENE *comes back and sits down.*]

IRENE: No, Louis.
LOUIS: These people, they break you by smiling at you one day and ignoring you the next, by their hateful toleration, by crossing the damn road when they see the two of us coming.
>[*Pause.*]

> You people are such good dancers
> We bet you're good in bed
> We bet you're also good runners
> But you don't have much in your heads.

IRENE: They don't say that any more, though.
LOUIS: It's older than the national anthem.
>[*Pause.*]

> It is the national anthem.
>[*Pause.*]

> In those first few weeks I used to go for long walks past buildings that looked like they were closed. Everywhere looked like it was closed. Then I'd come a little closer and find they were really open, that there was light, and I used to go inside and find these dead people playing games on green tables, or drinking, or listening to greasy music, and asking me questions like, 'Is your father a King?', and 'Do you prefer eating white people or coloured people?', and in one of these open-closed places I met a man so lonely that everywhere he went he carried his suitcase with him just to remind him that one day he's soon going to be leaving this place.
>[*Pause.*]

> And then out again into the street where the lights are so bright that sometimes it looks clearer at night than in the day. And then it would start up again. The rain. The rain, slanting hail tearing at exposed flesh. When you can't afford a jacket or an overcoat even. And I

stop and think by the side of the road.
> [*Pause.*]

Do you know how long it is since I've seen the sea?
> [*Pause.*]

IRENE: Haven't you ever liked it here?

LOUIS: I lost my nerve. I don't fly close to the sun no more.
> [*Pause.*]

The lights of the Empire Cinema in Leicester Square. You can't believe what that means to a grown man from a small island where only six or seven houses have proper electricity. Two years ago Louis White stands outside a cinema and cries. A cinema, girl, not a Buckingham Palace or Houses of Parliament. A cinema. And the traffic lights, roundabouts, lampposts, chimney pots like skyscrapers to me, and people pouring down the streets at the end of the day|like it's World War Two about to break out again. And me hiding in shop doorways scared out of my mind, girl. Taking shelter in a shop doorway in Oxford Street.
> [*Pause.*]

I'm writing such rich letters back home. Even British Railways smelt sweet that first year and when she left me for the fisherman I just wrote and told her good luck. No hard feelings, no regrets. I'm upset, for the girl was something to me but no regrets. I'm in England. The earth is a platform not an anchor to a man like me.

IRENE: I remember you saying that.

LOUIS: You don't remember for when I made it up I had never met you as yet.

IRENE: I remember you telling me, though. When we first met in that awful club.

LOUIS: The 'Z' club.

IRENE: I could see it was starting to get to you then.

LOUIS: No. Nothing bothered me in those days.

IRENE: It did, Louis. You know it did.

LOUIS: You think I'm different from a white man?
[*Pause.*]
Better and less in one?
IRENE: Of course you're different. You're different from any man.
LOUIS: I think I know why they look at us.
IRENE: It doesn't matter.
LOUIS: So they can cry 'progress' and vomit at the same time.
[*Pause.*]
IRENE: Don't let it get to you. Not now.
LOUIS: I want to go.
IRENE: Where?
LOUIS: I don't know.
IRENE: Finish your drink first.
[*Pause.*]
LOUIS: If you feel safe with me why do you always look so fearful when coloured people, especially coloured women, look at you?
[*Pause.*]
I notice how you look, you know. Your eyes dropping slightly, your face making an aimless smile, your grip tightening in my hand, or on my leg.
IRENE: I'm not afraid.
[*Pause.*]
LOUIS: I feel the same way sometimes. Hurts, makes you feel foolish for a minute.
[*Pause.*]
I look around and wonder how many road accidents we're going to cause today.
[*Pause.*]
It's us who these white people are going to riot about.
IRENE: Why?
LOUIS: Nigger and nigger-lover. They don't really hate the coloured man with a brick in one hand and terror in his eyes for they're used to that from slavery days.

Act Two

What they are not used to is a coloured man with a white woman on one arm and a spring in his step.

[*Pause.*]

We've done it, Irene.

IRENE: Done what?

LOUIS: Turned over our hostages to fortune... in England.

[*He laughs.*]

Look at them. These people here who make you feel safe. You know what they think of you? Pervert. Easy screw. Whore. Black man's white woman. She must have three breasts or bad breath or she fucked the West Indian cricket team on their last tour or her father must have fucked her when she was a child and that made her go funny.

[*Pause. He laughs.*]

Whore. Whore. Whore.

IRENE: I know what they say! I know what they think!

LOUIS: And you can live with it? You're happy to live like that?

IRENE: I can only live with it if you can. I can't do it if you keep saying all this, nobody can.

LOUIS: I want to go home.

IRENE: Then let's go home.

LOUIS: No. I mean home, home. Back home.

IRENE: I see.

[*Pause.*]

LOUIS: Depression is eating me out, Irene.

IRENE: I know.

[*Pause.*]

LOUIS: I want to go home alone.

IRENE: I'll give you what money I have if it'll help.

LOUIS: No. You'll need it.

IRENE: Come home with me tonight but don't just go in the middle of the night again. Wait till morning then you can go. I won't try to stop you.

[*Pause.*]

LOUIS: I have to go for I just don't like what is happening to me here.
> [*Pause.*]

IRENE: Do you hate me?

LOUIS: I don't hate.
> [*Pause.*]
>
> Are you with them?

IRENE: With who?

LOUIS: Them.
> [*He points at the other people in the pub. Pause.*]
>
> Or are you with me?

IRENE: I want to be with you.

LOUIS: For the baby's sake?

IRENE: I had to tell you last night. I mean, you had to know sometime, didn't you? Didn't you?
> [*Pause.*]
>
> You're more important to me than the baby.

LOUIS: I don't want you.
> [*Pause.*]
>
> I can't afford the butler.
> [*Pause.*]
>
> I don't mean it.
> [*Pause.*]
>
> I don't know if you talk to them about me. I don't know if you see the teeth behind their smile. I should never have touched you. I should never have come to play amongst the hibiscus.
> [IRENE *reaches over to touch him.*]
>
> Don't touch me, Irene.
> [*Pause.* IRENE *stands up.*]

IRENE: I'm going now, if that's what you want.
> [LOUIS *looks away.*]
>
> I said I'm going now.
> [*Pause.*]
>
> Louis?
> [*Pause.*]

Louis, if you don't want the baby I can always get rid of it.

> [*He looks up at her.*]

But I won't.

> [*Pause.*]

You don't have to see me again.

> [*Pause.*]

I'm used to being on my own.

> [*She begins to cry.*]

I'm not much use to you any more, am I?

LOUIS: Use?

IRENE: But at least I can still fight. The right things.

> [*Pause.*]

I won't forget you.

LOUIS: You're not going to forget me?

IRENE: I'm not... no, it doesn't matter.

LOUIS: Of course it matters. Everything matters in this country. Dirty milk-bottles matter. Raggedy pants on a washing line matter.

> [IRENE *bends forward and kisses* LOUIS *on the cheek.*]

IRENE: Goodbye, Louis.

LOUIS: They're still watching.

IRENE: I know they are but it doesn't matter. It really doesn't matter.

> [*His eyes follow her across the floor and out of the pub. The jukebox heaves itself to life again and he takes a drink and looks nervously around.*]

> [*Lights fade.*]

THE END

Also available from Amber Lane Press

CARYL PHILLIPS   *Strange Fruit*

Strange Fruit is a powerful study of a black family caught between two cultures. Vivien Marshall, a schoolteacher, has been alone in England with her two sons, Alvin and Errol, for over twenty years. But, despite their education, and her lifelong hopes of them making it in the mother-country, a schism has developed, which is further aggravated when Alvin returns to England after attending his grandfather's funeral in the Caribbean. Drawn into this family conflict are two other characters: Vernice, Vivien's neighbour and friend from the West Indies, and Shelley, Errol's English girlfriend.

CARYL PHILLIPS   *Where There is Darkness*

Where There is Darkness examines the plight of a West Indian man, Albert Williams, on the eve of his return to the Caribbean after an absence of 25 years. After a farewell party at his house he faces the reality of what his time in Britain has meant to him, his family and friends.

Amber Lane Press publishes an extensive range of contemporary plays. Ask your bookseller about other available titles, or write or telephone for a current catalogue.

Amber Lane Press, 9 Middle Way, Oxford OX2 7LH.
Tel. Oxford (0865) 50545